BLACK PAPER ALBUM

poems

by

KAREN SCHULTE

Finishing Line Press
Georgetown, Kentucky

BLACK PAPER ALBUM

poems

Copyright © 2023 by Karen Schulte
ISBN 979-8-88838-138-0 First Edition
All rights reserved under International and Pan-American Copyright Conventions. No part of this book may be reproduced in any manner whatsoever without written permission from the publisher, except in the case of brief quotations embodied in critical articles and reviews.

ACKNOWLEDGMENTS

I wish to thank:
Bard's Annual Anthologies, which has published many of my poems, among them, "Rembrandt's Camera" in their Anthology of 2020.
"Black Paper Album," was published in Paumanok, Transition, 2023
"Wild Berries in Sullivan County" was published in *Suffolk County Poetry Review*, 2019.
"Summer Ice" and "At the Edge" were published in my book of collected poems, "Where Desire Settles," 2016.

My special thanks to the poetry community on Long Island, NY for their encouragement, guidance, and especially to Gladys Henderson, Poet Laureate of Suffolk County 2017-2019 whose expertise and poetic spirit guided me throughout this book.

Publisher: Leah Huete de Maines
Editor: Christen Kincaid
Cover Art: Karen Schulte
Author Photo: Karen Schulte
Cover Design: Elizabeth Maines McCleavy

Order online: www.finishinglinepress.com
also available on amazon.com

Author inquiries and mail orders:
Finishing Line Press
PO Box 1626
Georgetown, Kentucky 40324
USA

Table of Contents

Black Paper Album 1

Defining Line 2

Alchemy 3

Picture Taking 4

Rembrandt's Camera 5

A Matter of Some Importance 6

Homeward 7

Summer Ice 8

At the Edge 9

Wild Berries 11

Catskill Synagogue 12

Lost Keys 14

Snapshot 15

Dance Lesson 16

Red Taffeta 17

Fault Lines 18

*For Eli with answers to questions
which lead to more questions*

"*And all the lives we ever lived and all the lives to be
are full of trees and changing leaves.*"
Virginia Woolf, To the Lighthouse

Black Paper Album

My fingers run over the crumbling edges
of black photo paper, the album's soft binding,
held together with hand-tied string, is coming apart.

Inside, fasteners have lost their grip,
the glue on the back of ancient snapshots fast disappearing.
Old photographs no longer secure fall, page after page,
a cascade of them from my father's youth.

He and his brothers stand arm in arm, in the courtyard
of their Hebrew orphanage, anchored to each other,
their own fortress against whatever lies ahead.

Turn more pages, more yellowed pictures fall.
The Twentieth Century moves on, becomes undone.
My mother's family, people I have forgotten or who have died
tumble out, no longer attached to time or place.

My mother with her slick bob, slim and fashionable,
leans against her parent's porch railing, looking pensive,
her sister sits in a wicker chair, pregnant and peaceful.

My uncles in soldier uniform, proud to be first generation
American, stare at me with pride, the youngest one play-acts
with his bayonet while smiling for the camera. Even pictures
of family dogs I have almost forgotten pose looking serene.

And for a while, we were— my father's brothers, my mother's family,
cousins I no longer see, even my brother, so young, swinging
his baseball bat with joy and vigor.

All these images are now between self-adhesive, acid-free pages
with new captions underneath securing them for a new century
bound to a different time with different sorrows
leaving remnants of the past with traces of the future.

Defining Line: The "Oblast"

My father never talked about his family,
or what he knew about their past along with
their last name, two syllables, short and hard,

bestowed upon them in Eastern Europe
by some official centuries back
when someone with a title
could determine who you were,

your name as well. Where once you were
known as a son or daughter of a father
whose bloodline went back generations
with nothing to add until change came

with a single stroke of the pen—
as random as playing cards, rolling dice,
adding a surname where there was none,
reversing perspective top to bottom.

In my ancestor's case, it was a bloodless,
shifting thing, a line, an "oblast"
separating one province from another,
one town from the next.

Six letters, easy to remember,
only erasable to those who make the rules—
an identification as stark as piles of stones
along barbed-wire fences.

With little more than their bodies,
before actions became a noose,
they crossed armed borders and barricades
to find whatever was possible—

a warm bed, food in a bowl, walls
that didn't shake when soldiers walked by.

Alchemy

They stand next to each other in this old photograph,
separated by inches exactly the same from top to bottom
as if tailor made by an invisible marker. They look
straight at the camera, smiling and proud in their
best clothes waiting for a celebration.

That is how I remember them, side by side,
never touching, at least never seen by me.
At home, even their beds were narrow twins
with a night table and two lamps between,
a bedroom for roommates not a long-married couple.

My grandfather, tall and slim,
handsome with a shock of white hair.
Grandma, at his side, short and round,
never at a loss for words, in Yiddish
or any other language she could muster.

They seem to have lived in two separate worlds
while together in one: there was some rumor
their marriage was an arrangement. It may have
been so but they appear to be content.

Whatever they had, it was more than they
bargained for at a time when there was no way
of knowing what lies ahead when you
cross an ocean as wide as the Atlantic.

But here they stand posed together
as inexplicable as if they landed on Mars
flung from some dying planet
to a place they could never imagine—

where a sideways glance and grit could turn dross
to gold or an ordinary stone to something like marble.

Picture Taking

There is sadness
in my mother's eyes,
a sorrow caught by the camera
held by my father
taken in
black and white,
a snapshot, one of many
still sharp
with her image.

My father, in another
looks exhausted
but resigned,
sits on a park bench
holding me propped beside him
wrapped in my baby bunting blanket
waiting for my mother
and the perfect moment
she'll take my picture.

Somewhere in these photos
is the clue
to what came after—
when I was no longer the center
and driving spoke of a wheel,
always turning
in the same groove

unaware of the cyclical force
of the past,
my parent's fears,
memories I knew nothing of—
only the thrill that day,
held high above my father's knee
with a look on my face
of exuberant joy,
or a rush, perhaps
of terror

Rembrandt's Camera

A bonnet hides my face
tilted upward in this portrait
of my three-year-old self
seated on a bench outside
my grandfather's store.

My grandfather sits at one end,
his white spitz dog
in between,
lit against deepening shadows,
an illumination worthy
of an artist of light and shade.

Grandpa with his white wavy hair
looks straight ahead.
On his lips, a smile
about to happen, stopped
short by some thought
he could only
reveal to himself.

Rembrandt would have been
proud to paint us—
my grandfather with his first American grandchild,
but it was only my father
taking pictures whenever he could
who pointed that box camera
at the precise moment
and snapped us
sitting so peacefully.

A Matter of Some Importance

Whatever could I be saying
wagging my finger at another child

About a year or two older
or at least a head taller

Both of us in profile
faces obscured by bonnets

Next to grandpa's store
down the hill from main street

Deep in discussion
with an urgency I have yet to outgrow

Or so it seems from a lifetime
of hits and misses

But at three or four years old
I can only guess

From the image of two children
one looking up, the other down

Engrossed in a deep matter
of solving some problem

In our warm clothes with parents
close by taking our pictures

With not much to worry about
except to wonder

If the next train to roll over the tracks
would be on time at 3 O'clock

And would the engineer wave to us
as it passed?

Homeward

There are three hills
in my mother's hometown,
one in the village rose straight
up from level ground
past my grandparents' home
to become a high, steep hill
we never climbed. Then there
was the one careening down Broadway
past grandpa's tavern disappearing
at the railroad tracks.

The third hill, I remember best:
it led out of the village proper
to my Aunt's house, its highway
curving snakelike
around bends of woodland,
wild flowers and weeds
on the way to the town center.

Climbing that hill
was the only way my cousins and I
could visit each other on summer days
before car rides ferried us
back and forth in style.

We walked uphill, in an uneven line,
talked little, aware of our feet
on rocky ground, careful of cars passing,
as we were homeward bound
and knew, even then,
as we trudged upward,
how special it was to be going somewhere
where your presence was valued
and you were held dear,
dearer than anything you
could wish for, with little
or nothing to be said.

Summer Ice

We were always together come summer
in the white house on a sloping hill
in a village no longer there,
days when all there was to do
was gather around the kitchen table
five small children in mid-morning glare,
fine dust gathering overhead
while my Aunt Esther's manicured hands
whisked milk, eggs and sugar
in a bowl until thickened,
the cream, round and deep,
ready for the freezer, until pure
vanilla ice cream, iced for our spoons
to scrape the surface, soft enough
for the tasting—even the white liquid,
melted on the bottom was scooped
into our mouths, sweetly thickened,
it rolled off our tongues to our lips and chins,
much of it on clothes and fingers,
weighing us down until we collapsed,
became anchored in spirit and bone,
slept like the children we were,
wrapped in our own measured breathing.

At the Edge

Crossing the George Washington Bridge
driving along the old Route 17
my father rolled the chrome green Chevy
through the biting winds of late November's
Thanksgiving Day weekend
with a precision of grave concentration.
The twists in the road
along the two lane highway
became narrower, my father,
then my mother fell silent.
The radio went dim to a dull hum
as my mother squinted her eyes
looking for the turn-off
on the far side of the hills,
her childhood stretching before her,
not always welcoming, but she knew
those turns around the bend
just where the river came into view,
shrouded that day by a fog so thick
memory only worked until it didn't.
The curve was sudden, the drop
from the precipice deep, headlights
separated into small pinpoints—
nothing could be seen to guide us
leaving two children cowering,
my mother clinging to her seat.
Almost at the guardrail my father
hit the brakes and stopped the car's
onward slide to the valley below,
its hills wrapped in darkening halos,
when all we could do was sit in fear
unable to see the plunge,
imagine falling into thick, soggy mist,
feel the numbness of body and soul
suddenly finding ourselves
secure in our seats, the wilderness

behind us, never talking about
what almost happened except in
the backdrop of interrupted dreams
before we pushed on in silence
traveling further than we wanted to go.

Wild Berries in Sullivan County

In the late days of August, before dawn,
my aunt would wake me, hurry me along,
get a pail for herself, a smaller one for me,
and we would climb in the old Studebaker,
with the sun just rising, drive a few miles from her home
to a neighbor's woods to pick wild blackberries.

Me, in loose jeans, my aunt's dress billowing,
my hair slick and drawn tight
into two crisp braids down to my waist,
my aunt, blond hair tucked under
her straw bonnet, takes me on a path
of low lying bushes drooping with blackberries,
ripening in the haze of early morning.

I never minded the sharp nettles,
the low branches grabbing my feet,
the black ink from the berries smeared
on my face or blouse, tapestry
gone wild on everything I touched,
my skin, my hands, all purple,
a color I didn't expect, not from its rouge dakness.

My aunt praised me for my diligence, my concentration,
and I was proud she picked me, not her own children,
all blond and fair, whose skin would burn and peel
from hours in the sun, but not mine—
glowing with the sweat of labor,
the smell of open fields, the sweetness of the fruit,
the sun lopsided in the sky, stunned by its persistence.

Catskill Synagogue

When I think of that summer
so many years ago spent in
the foothills of the Catskills
when I was only eleven or twelve
trying to understand who I was
where I came from
where I was going
The thread of past to present
began in my grandparent's
village but it could be
elsewhere, someplace in
Russia, Poland, Ukraine
with no name to speak of
a shtetl in some dusty countryside
with a synagogue much like
the one in this village
across the street from
where we lived—
where it rose from its foundation
like a misplaced great gull
sitting on its sun-baked nest
ready to rise up, take flight
disappear in dust and mica
but stayed in place
leaving ten old men
praying before the bimah
in a language I didn't understand
all long vowels and pauses sung
in unison, sometimes alone
always, the prayerbook before them
I held as well but could not read—
those inked letters with long curlicues
of dots and flourishes, of slanted lines
curved upward beseeching
the Almighty's blessings
chanted each day

as if they first heard it
bodies bent low, bowing
deep before rising.

Lost Keys

My mother didn't look back
        she just kept climbing

up the fire escape ladder
        leaving me below
        holding her shopping bag

wondering what to do next
        if I had to

but I was only five or four
        and knew nothing

remained riveted to the spot
        where I stood

watched as she worked her way up
        slowly, deliberately

steadying herself on her brown scuffed pumps
        one narrow tread after another

on those tapered strips of rusted metal
        three stories up
        never looking down

before she lifted the bedroom window
        let herself drop
        over the edge

wave to me from inside
        to come home the proper way
        through the vestibule, up heavy stairs

while she retrieved her keys
        cool in the palm of her hand.

Snapshot

We didn't know life was risky
taking us where we didn't want
to go especially when you know
only one place day after day
as the three girls did when
my father took our picture
in the late '40's holding
our baby dolls in front of us.
I am in the middle, two of
the older girls on each side—
we smile broadly for the camera,
sure of ourselves, of our future
as it continues from the past,
without sorrow, without regrets,
not knowing one of us will be gone
a decade later. Stunned into silence
by what was least expected,
we mourned for the girl
and her children left behind,
most of all ourselves
our futures no longer clear,
the story line broken,
nothing was straight and narrow
but how we longed to keep
our little circle
of friends and neighbors
close enough to join hands
march into the wilderness
saying "hello" "goodbye"
over and over,
knowing it cannot last
as we muddle through
days and months of trying
to hold on, leading back
to each other, not as it was,
in the fleeting slide of yesteryear
but what it still could be
again in our own time

Dance Lessons

Once a week riding the D train a group
of thirteen year old girls from uptown
serious and determined, dance bags slung
over shoulders, leotards and leggings
coiled in neat rolls,

travel underground with a purpose,
almost an hour to West Fourth St.,
walk past Broadway to a squat brick building
whose cage-like elevator carries them to a bare studio,

its battered piano in a corner, students warming up
cross-legged on a gleaming wooden floor,
others at the barre wait to take seated positions
for the teacher's ceaseless counts of

"contract, release, spiral and fall…and one, and two"

over again until it seeps into their very being.
They bend and rotate positions, move according to space,
bodies intuitive, fluid, lean and persistent
push against gravity aware each pose
tells a story, pound it into muscle and spine,

pour grace and strength into every inch of concentration,
gather all they can of speed and desire,
inhale deeply, glide through thin air
until grounded…centered…still.

Red Taffeta

The girl in the red taffeta dress
perches on a flowered armchair
in a well draped living room.
It holds her smiling image:
the dress curled above her knees,
white crinoline slip
flouncing underneath.

At sixteen, she knows
she outshines her mother
who is somewhere beyond her vision
watching her posing
for the camera.

She thinks she is lovely
but unsure. Her red lips,
dark hair gleam with possibility
foreign to her but not to others.

Staring into the camera,
she smiles because she is told to.
When she finally stands,
the dress flares from her waist,
moves with the motion of her hips.

She will remember this day,
not because it's a brother's bar mitzvah
but as a moment anchored in
yesterday's tales she no longer
believes and chooses to ignore.

Mostly, she'll remember the sway
of the dress against her hips,
fifties music blaring forth,
his hand on the small of her back

siding down, and the piercing look
in her mother's eyes

Fault Lines

The child she once was
thought her world
would end in fire—

She feared the frayed wire,
lit match, burning pot
until she put

her mind to other things
grew into her young body,
found herself immersed

in everyday routine,
grownup struggles
moving along fault lines

hidden so deep
with bits and pieces of debris
from the past, barely visible

leaving traces of lost causes, old griefs
whose shadows stretch long
and everlasting.

Karen Schulte is a retired social worker/therapist who began writing in grade school, managed to win a New York Citywide writing contest that paid her way through college, and continued writing seriously after retirement. She has had her poetry published in a number of journals and anthologies including *Long Island Quarterly, Poetica Magazine, Paterson Review, Bards Annual Anthology, PPA Literary Review, NCPL Literary Review*. Her first collection of poems, "Where Desire Settles," won first place in the *Writer's Digest* 2017 Annual Contest for a self-published book of poetry.

www.ingramcontent.com/pod-product-compliance
Lightning Source LLC
Chambersburg PA
CBHW022129090426
42743CB00008B/1071